LIVE ADVENT
at Home

Daily Prayers and Activities
for FAMILIES

Patricia Mathson

Liguori
LIGUORI, MISSOURI

Imprimi Potest: Harry Grile, CSsR
Provincial, Denver Province, The Redemptorists

Published by Liguori Publications
Liguori, Missouri 63057
To order, call 800-325-9521
liguori.org

Library of Congress Cataloging-in-Publication Data to come

Mathson, Patricia L.
    Live Advent at home : daily prayers and activities for families / Patricia Mathson. —
1st ed.
        p. cm.
    ISBN 978-0-7648-2035-9
    1. Advent—Prayers and devotions. 2. Families—Prayers and devotions. 3. Catholic Church—Prayers and devotions. I. Title.
    BX2170.A4M38 2011
    242'.645—dc22

                                                              2011005733

Liguori Publications, a nonprofit corporation, is an apostolate of the Redemptorists. To learn more about the Redemptorists, visit Redemptorists.com

Printed in the United States of America
15 14 13 12 11 / 5 4 3 2 1
First Edition

Contents

Introduction

Our journey through the liturgical seasons of Advent and Christmas helps us realize all that God has done for us. As we begin a new church year, we are able to start anew, knowing that Emmanuel has come, and God is with us.

This special time of year offers our families the opportunity to make time for what is most important in the midst of our busy lives. Even with all of the events and commitments that crowd this season, family faith-sharing can form an integral part of preparing for the great celebration of Christmas.

This easy-to-use book will help families walk together through the season of Advent and into the season of Christmas. The journey begins with the first Sunday of Advent and continues through the feast of Epiphany. This prac-tical book will help your family live the hope of Advent and the joy of Christmas together, year after year.

Each week begins with a reflection on the Sunday Gospels you may hear in Mass. Since the readings differ each year based upon the *Lectionary* cycles, we reflect here on the major themes of each of the readings. You can deepen your family's understanding of the Gospels by sharing these reflections right before or right after you celebrate Sunday Mass together.

Each day of the journey has its own page, containing a reflection, sharing question, activity, and prayer. The short reflection is to focus your family on the spirit of the seasons. Talk about the sharing question as a family and think about it as you go about your day. The daily activity is a way to help you bring the season to life as a family, while the activity pages for each week are meant to bring fun in the spirit of the season to your family. The daily prayer will help you pray together each day as you journey to Bethlehem and beyond. Also included are family prayers for the Advent and Christmas seasons. Consider learning and praying these prayers together as well in a way that works for your needs.

This book is for families of all shapes and sizes. It is a book for families just getting started with faith sharing and families who have been doing this a long time. It is for parents, grandparents, and extended families. It is an opportunity for your family or extended family to share faith across generations.

The ideas in this book will help families connect with the God who is already here in our lives, our homes, and our world. Many different types of activities are offered to appeal to a wide variety of families of all ages and stages. So use this resource in whatever

way makes sense for your own family. Do what you can as your family's schedule permits. This book can be shared at dinner time, at bedtime, in the morning, at breakfast, at lunch, after school, in the evening or whenever your family gathers. Actively involve individual family members by inviting them to read aloud the day's prayer or to participate in other ways.

This book can also be a resource for faith-sharing with other families if you gather together during these holy seasons. Do the page together for the day on which your group meets. On other days use the appropriate pages at home until it is time to meet again. This allows for faith sharing with other families and within your own family.

May God bless you as you walk your journey through Advent and Christmas as a family together. Each family is different and each experience will be different. But everyone can share hope in an awesome God, hope in the future, and hope in one another. Come, Lord Jesus!

Family Prayer

Lord Jesus Christ,
we give you thanks for your love
for each of us during Advent and always.
May this season be a time of new beginnings
for our family as we begin a new church year.

Show our family how to live in hope
during this holy season of Advent.
Help us to share our thoughts, our joys,
and our struggles with one another.

May we follow you always as the light
of the world and the light of our lives.
Guide our family during this season of Advent
and teach us to share your love with others.

Help us to be people of compassion
who look beyond our own family
to make a difference in the lives of others
through our words and actions.

We ask your blessing on our family
this day and all through the Advent season.
As we journey together toward Bethlehem,
may we walk in faith, hope, and love.
Come, Lord Jesus!

Amen.

First Week of Advent

During Advent we get ready to celebrate the coming of Jesus as a baby in a manger at Bethlehem. But we also remember that Christ is present in our lives today, and we are joyfully waiting for his coming at the end of time. What we do while we are waiting for Jesus is important. In the Gospels this week, Jesus speaks to us of being ready. We are reminded not to put off doing the right thing so that we are always prepared for God's coming. We can get ready for Jesus' coming at Christmas by allowing Advent to make a difference in our lives each and every day.

Therefore, stay awake! For you do not know on which day your Lord will come. So, too, you also must be prepared. Matthew 24:42, 44

The Gospels urge us to look at our priorities. By his words and actions, Jesus showed us that we are to care the most about people in need—the poor, the lost, the homeless, the sick, and all who need our help—be-

Let us walk in the light of the LORD.

ISAIAH 2:5

fore we care about ourselves. If we are to live as followers of Jesus Christ during Advent, we must measure what we do against his example. We are to open our hearts to be people of compassion as Jesus was.

Are we spending too much time on what is not important to God, or could we do more to serve others?

"Be watchful! Be alert! You do not know when the time will come" (Mark 13:33).

How often do we say, I'll take time to reach out to others when I'm not so busy, when I don't have so much going on, or when work or school aren't taking up so much time. But the truth is, we can usually make time for what is important if we make it a priority. We always have time to watch for God. Jesus speaks to our hearts in the words of the Gospels, reminding us to make serving God and others an important part of our lives. After all, this is how we prepare for Jesus' coming.

How can we make time in our busy lives for serving God and others?

"Beware that your hearts do not become drowsy from…the anxieties of daily life, and that day catch you by surprise…be vigilant at all times and pray…" (Luke 21:34, 36).

Advent is a time of new beginnings. This season is the start of a new church year. We have another opportunity to begin anew and do it right, even if the worries of daily life get us down. We can live in love of God and others each day of Advent and beyond.

What are some ways we can show our love for God and others this Advent?

Walk in the Light

Advent reflection

Have you ever been afraid in the dark? When it's dark in the night, we wait for the light of morning. When the day is dark and rainy, we wait to see the sun come out. We need light in our lives and in our hearts.

In the season of Advent, we are called as a family to walk in the light of Jesus Christ. We leave the darkness behind and walk toward the light of Jesus at Bethlehem. We wait for the coming of Christ as the light of the world. We wait as the people of Israel waited for a Savior.

As we journey toward the celebration of Christmas, we can walk together into the light. May the light of Christ shine in our hearts and in our lives during this season of Advent and always.

Advent question

✦ What is one way our family can walk in the light of Christ during Advent?

Advent activity

Look around the church after Mass today and see what signs of the Advent season you can find.

✦ Is there an Advent wreath?
✦ How many candles are on it?
✦ Does your church have banners or other decorations for Advent?
✦ What is the color of the Advent decorations?
✦ Does your parish have Advent prayer cards or other resources to take home?

 ## Advent prayer

Lord Jesus Christ,
we pray that you will be with our family
as we begin our Advent journey together.
You are the light that shines in the darkness
and the light that we are to follow.
Watch over us and guide each of us
that we may walk in the light of your love.
Amen.

9

Wait for Jesus

Advent reflection

Is it difficult to wait for a birthday party or for someone to visit you? Advent is a time of waiting. As we wait to celebrate Christmas, we remember how much God loves us.

"Advent" means coming. During Advent, we get ready for the coming of Christmas and our celebration of the birth of Jesus. We wait in joyful hope because we know that God has sent Jesus to us. We know that Advent leads us to Christmas.

The season of Advent offers opportunities for our family to celebrate the good things in our lives and in our world. We can choose to focus on what is positive in a world that sometimes seems to focus on the negative. In this way we live the spirit of hope of the season of Advent and live as Advent people.

Advent question

✦ How can our family live in hope and discover the good in our lives during this Advent?

Advent activity

Some days are difficult, but there is always something for which we can be thankful if we look hard enough. We should look for the positive, not the negative. Sometimes what one person sees as the best part of the day may surprise other family members.

Ask each family member to share one good thing that happened to him or her today. Consider making this a daily practice around the family meal table.

Advent prayer

God of every good thing,
we wait in joyful hope to celebrate
the coming of our Lord Jesus Christ.
We ask your blessing on our family
during this holy Advent season
that we may live always as your people.
Amen.

10

Remember God's Promise

Advent reflection

Did anyone ever break a promise to you? Sometimes people don't keep the promises they make. That's not the way it is with God. We know that God always keeps promises to us. God promised to send the people a Savior and kept this promise in a way no one could have expected.

The season of Advent is an opportunity for our family to choose to live the faith we have in our awesome God. We can either try to live up to what we think others expect of us or we can remember that it is God who gives us life and purpose by keeping his promises for our lives. We should choose to trust God's promises.

We can look into our hearts and our lives and see God's promise of love reflected there. We can also see God's love in one another. By being loving in our words and our actions, we live the spirit of the Advent season.

Advent question

✦ How Advent make a difference in our lives?

Advent activity

This Advent, see how we can share God's love with others in our daily lives. As a family, Let's name some opportunities we have to help one another. These could include: lending a hand with a difficult project, listening to someone who is having a tough day, saying hello to a new person at school or work, or waiting patiently in line at a store. What are some other ways each of us has to brighten someone's day?

Advent prayer

Awesome God,
we give you thanks and praise
for all that you have done for us.
Guide our family that we may
live as Advent people.
Help us open our hearts
and our lives to the needs of others.
Amen.

Pray in All Things

Advent reflection

Do you email or call a good friend often? It is important to keep in touch with friends, and it is important to keep in touch with God. Prayer connects us with God and with one another. Prayer is part of our relationship with God.

Prayer is important during the season of Advent. We pray to God as we prepare to celebrate the great miracle of Christmas. We give praise to God for all that God has done for us. We ask God's help each day because with God all things are possible.

Advent is a time when we are called to pray for the needs of others. We can pray together as a family for other people. The Advent season reminds us of how we should be living all through the year, as people of prayer.

Advent question

+ How can our family make more time for prayer during Advent?

Advent activity

Sometimes we only pray for what we need or what our family needs, but we should also remember to pray for the needs of other people. This is a difficult time of year for many people. We should remember those who are suffering in our prayers and share God's love with them.

As a family, let's pray for those for whom Advent is a struggle due to poverty, illness, or grief. A family member can begin the prayer with the sign of the cross and by reading the prayer below. Then, each person can offer a person or group of people for whom they'd like to pray during our special prayer time. Finally, the leader can conclude with "Amen."

Advent prayer

Lord God,
we give you praise for all that you are
and all that you have done for us.
During Advent help our family
make time for prayer in our busy lives.
May we live our faith in you
in all we do and say each day.
Amen.

12

Make Good Choices

Advent reflection

Is it easy to make good choices? During Advent we are called to make good choices in our lives. We can choose to live the Advent season as a time of rushing around and trying to get it all done, or we can choose to take time for what is important.

We are given the gift of each day by God and the gift of the season of Advent by our Church. We can make choices based on what we think others expect of us. Or we can make choices that help us live the life for which we were created by God.

It's up to our family how we live the gift of the Advent season in our lives. During Advent let us look deep into our hearts and find the courage and the strength to follow God's will.

Advent question

✦ How do our choices during Advent reflect our faith
  in Jesus Christ?

Advent activity

Think about the gift of time this Advent, and discuss these questions together as a family.

✦ Is there a way to make time to live Advent as a family?
✦ Is there one thing that we can let go of in order to have time to share, time to pray, and time to praise God?
✦ What would that be?
✦ What could we do with that time to live Advent?

Advent prayer

God, Father and Creator,
we ask you to walk with our family
on our journey through the Advent season.
Empower us to make good choices
and make time for what is important.
We wait for the coming of Jesus Christ,
who is the light of the world for all people.
Amen.

Reach Out a Helping Hand

Advent reflection

Do we judge people by the outside or the inside? God calls us to care about other people as Jesus showed us. Jesus called us to see each person as God's creation. We should treat all people with respect.

We are responsible for others and are responsible for making good choices that show that we see and love Jesus in our neighbors.

Sometimes we do not see Jesus in the faces of others. During Advent our family should try to see Jesus Christ in a lonely neighbor, a hungry child, a sick person, or someone who is homeless. We can make a difference, one person at a time.

Advent question

✦ What is one way our family can reach out a helping hand during Advent?

Advent activity

God calls us to make a difference in the lives of others. Let's find a way for our family to concretely help those in need. Can our family contribute extra items to the local food panty? Can we buy extra toothbrushes and toothpaste and donate them to a shelter? Can we visit an elderly person for an hour so the caregiver can have time off?

We can think of some other ways to serve others in the spirit of love of the Advent season. Let's choose one way for our family to make a difference in someone else's life and do it this week.

Advent prayer

Lord Jesus Christ,
open our hearts to the people around us
during this holy season of Advent.
Help our family to see your face in other people
and to follow your way of love for others.
May we make a difference in the life
of at least one person this day.
Amen.

Share a Time of Joy

Advent reflection

Were you ever really happy about something that happened to you or to one of your friends? Mary was happy for her cousin, Elizabeth. After Mary hears from the angel that her cousin was to have a baby, Mary goes to visit her. Certainly this was a joyful visit, as Mary looked forward to the birth of her own son, Jesus.

We know that Elizabeth's child grows up to be John the Baptist, a man who prepares the way for the public ministry of Jesus. We, too, wait in joyful hope for the coming of a Savior, as Mary did. We prepare our hearts and our lives for the coming of Jesus.

During the Advent season, we are filled with joy because we know that Christmas is only part of the story. We know that Christmas leads to Easter and new life for all of us.

Advent question

✦ How can our family share the joy of the Advent season with one another?

Advent activity

Sometimes we are nicer to friends than the people around us. We can find ways in our family life to show love and appreciation for our brothers and sisters and parents.

Let's show our love and appreciation for one another today by writing a short note such as "I love you," or, "Thanks for all you do." Then, we can surprise family members by putting the notes somewhere where they will find it.

Advent prayer

God of the universe,
our family waits during Advent
to celebrate the coming of Jesus.
Help us prepare the way of the Lord
through our actions toward one another.
May your kingdom come for all people
now and forever.
Amen.

15

Bible Search

As we begin the season of Advent, one of the psalms that we pray together at Mass is Psalm 25. The words of the psalm give us the words to say what is in our hearts. We pray to the God who created us and who is with us always. This is a beautiful psalm that can be prayed at home, too.

Work together as a family to fill in the blanks with the words to this psalm, using the words below. These words are found in the Bible at Psalm 25:4–6. Then pray the psalm together. This is a good psalm for the Advent season and all through the year.

Make known to me your __ __ __ __ , LORD;

__ __ __ __ __ me your paths.

Guide me in your __ __ __ __ __ and teach me,

for you are __ __ __ my savior.

for you I __ __ __ __ all the long day,

because of your goodness, __ __ __ __ .

Remember your compassion and __ __ __ __ .

God	**teach**
love	**wait**
truth	**ways**
LORD	

Word Find

The readings of the first Sunday of Advent help us to begin our journey through the Advent season. We prepare our hearts and our lives for the coming of Jesus Christ as a child in a manger and the Savior for the world. We wait in joyful hope.

At the bottom of this page are words from the readings of the first Sunday of Advent. Work together as a family to find and circle as many words as you can. Hint: letters can be used in more than one word.

C	E	S	G	R	P	C	U	H	R	O	C	M	X	Y	U
A	U	R	L	I	G	H	T	G	J	Z	T	G	O	D	S
T	W	H	E	A	R	T	S	L	O	N	K	L	Q	U	N
J	E	S	U	S	E	D	G	N	U	P	E	O	P	L	E
S	S	N	B	N	R	C	F	B	R	V	S	R	K	O	P
I	O	P	C	O	M	I	N	G	N	X	I	Y	T	R	G
G	N	I	A	W	E	S	O	M	E	K	S	I	L	N	S
N	L	A	W	A	K	E	G	B	Y	L	O	R	D	O	Q
S	N	R	B	G	I	Z	L	Q	P	O	L	P	U	R	T

COMING	JOURNEY	LIGHT
LORD	AWAKE	SIGNS
GOD	PEOPLE	GLORY
JESUS	HEARTS	AWESOME

Second Week of Advent

In the Gospels this week, we hear the story of John the Baptist preaching to the people. They tell us that John fulfills what the prophet Isaiah had said. John comes out of the wilderness to prepare the way for Jesus and his public ministry to the people. We, too, are to listen to John the Baptist today as we prepare our hearts for Jesus' coming.

"It was of him that the prophet Isaiah had spoken when he said: 'A voice of one crying out in the desert, prepare the way of the Lord, make straight his paths'" (Matthew 3:3).

Prepare the way of the LORD.

ISAIAH 40:3

The words of Isaiah are not only about John. These are words that speak to us during Advent. We are called to prepare the way of the Lord in our hearts and lives as we get ready to celebrate Christmas.

What are some ways we can prepare the way of the Lord in our hearts and lives as a family?

18

"One mightier than I is coming after me. I am not worthy to stoop and loosen the thongs of his sandals" (Mark 1:7).

John makes it clear to the people that he is only the messenger. John shares the good news of Jesus with others, and we are called to do the same through our words and actions. As a Church we are to point the way to Christ for others. They must be able to learn that Jesus is compassionate and loving by our caring words and actions. We are to reach out to other people as Jesus taught us.

"How can we share the good news of Jesus with other people?

John went throughout the whole region of the Jordan, proclaiming a baptism of repentance for the forgiveness of sins" (Luke 3:3).

John calls on people to repent and to be baptized. Most of us have already been baptized, but we can still learn from John. We all are called to change our hearts and turn our lives toward God to get ready to celebrate the coming of the Lord at Christmas. This is a tall order! But we must remember that all we are and all we do comes to us from the God who created us. With God all things are possible.

What does it mean to change our hearts and turn our lives toward God?

Give Thanks and Praise to God

Advent reflection

Is it important to thank someone who helps you? We should say thank you to God, too. God works miracles in our world each day. We see God's presence in the beauty of a sunrise, in the wonder of the universe, and in the love that people show toward others.

This Advent season is an opportunity for our family to give thanks to God for all that God has done for us. God loves us with an unending love. God will always be with us and will never turn away from us.

As we walk through the season of Advent on our journey to Bethlehem, we should give thanks and praise to God. We can glorify God for all that God has done for our family and our world. Our God is an awesome God.

Advent question

+ How can our family give thanks and praise to God
  by our words and actions during Advent?

Advent activity

Sit down as a family and make one-of-a-kind Christmas cards to give to special people. Use a sheet of construction paper folded in half for each card. Decorate the front of the cards with drawings or colorful shapes cut from Christmas scrapbook paper. Print the words "Merry Christmas" on the front. On the inside include a message and sign your name. Give the cards to people you know.

Advent prayer

God of promise,
our family gives you thanks and praise
during this Advent season of hope.
You fulfilled your promise to the people
in a way we never could have imagined.
Thank you for sending Jesus to show us
that the way to you is the way of love.
Amen.

Get Ready to Welcome Jesus

Advent reflection

What are some ways we get ready for a big celebration? We need to get ready to celebrate Christmas by preparing our hearts and our lives to welcome Jesus.

We prepare not only to celebrate the coming of Jesus Christ at Christmas, but to celebrate the presence of the risen Christ among us, and the return of our Lord at the end of time. Advent and Christmas lead us from the manger to the cross and resurrection.

Our family can get ready to welcome Jesus by our words and actions during Advent. We are called to share the good news of Jesus Christ with others, and to welcome them into our lives. This is a season to live the Gospels as loving and welcoming people. We get ready for the coming of Jesus by what we do and what we say each day.

Advent question

✦ How can our family get ready to welcome the Lord during Advent?

Advent activity

Brainstorm a list of some ways to live Advent as a family. Think of ideas to become more loving and welcoming, such as: pray together for the needs of others, go to an Advent program at church, give items through the parish giving-tree project, or make cookies and take them to a neighbor. Have someone write down all of the ideas. Then, as a family, choose one thing to do together to get ready to welcome Jesus.

 ## Advent prayer

Lord Jesus Christ,
help us to be like John the Baptist
and prepare to celebrate your coming.
Open our eyes to what is important in life
and open our hearts to the message of the Gospel.
May our family live the spirit of Advent
By welcoming others in our hearts and our lives.
Amen.

Follow the Example of Mary

Advent reflection

What are some things that we say yes to? When the angel Gabriel appeared to her and told her that she would be the mother of God's own son, Mary said yes to God. As we journey through the Advent season, we wait as Mary waited for the angel's words to be fulfilled.

Mary was faithful to God in all things, even when it was difficult. Her baby was born in a stable. She and Joseph had to flee to Egypt with baby Jesus. Later she saw people turn against her Son and nail him to the cross. We must be faithful to God in all times and places of our lives as Mary was in hers.

We can ask Mary to pray for our family to God. Mary is not only the mother of Jesus, but the mother of all of us. She is a sign of hope for us and for our world. The birth of Jesus who was not only God, but human just like us, is a sign of God's love for all of us. God has come to be with us, just as God was with Mary!

Advent question

✦ How can we say yes to God as Mary did?

Advent activity

Read stories together about Mary from a children's Bible. Great stories include how Mary said yes to God when the angel Gabriel appeared, and when she went on a trip to visit her cousin, Elizabeth. When the story is over, we can ask Mary to pray to Jesus for us by praying the prayer below, or another favorite prayer to Mary.

Advent prayer

Mary,
we honor you as the Mother of God
and our holy mother, too.
You are an example for all of us
of how to be faithful to God.
We ask you to pray for our family
to your Son, our Lord Jesus Christ.
Amen.

Forgive Others

Advent reflection

Is it easy to forgive someone who has hurt you? God calls us to forgive others as God forgives us. We are to share God's forgiveness and peace with other people.

The season of Advent offers us a wonderful opportunity to forgive others. We are also called to ask someone to forgive us for our words or actions that have hurt them. We must do this even if it is difficult for us and even if the person who has hurt us does not ask our forgiveness. This season is also a time to let go of grudges. We hurt ourselves and others in our lives when we hold onto our anger.

Advent is a time to be peacemakers in our families, our communities, and our world. The first step to living in peace is forgiveness, and it leads to another step and another toward a more peaceful family, community, and world. As we seek peace in our own lives, we must also join our prayers for peace to the prayers of people all over the world.

Advent question

✦ Why is it important for us to forgive others?

Advent activity

Each of us has opportunities to make a difference. We can try just for one day to get along with someone who is difficult or to speak positively to another person. We should use peaceful words and gestures instead of angry words.

Let's talk about ways our family can live as peacemakers. We can choose one way our family can live as peacemakers and do it this week.

Advent prayer

God of love,
we know that you are a God
who forgives us when we are wrong.
Give us the strength this Advent season
to forgive people who have hurt us
and let go of grudges against others.
We ask this in the name of Jesus.
Amen.

Take Time to Be Grateful

Advent reflection

Do you ever stop to count your blessings? Advent offers our family an opportunity to tell God that we are grateful for all that God has done for us.

There are many people who are blessings in our lives. We can thank these special people ourselves for all they have done for us, just as we thank God for the many ways they bless our lives. When we tell people that they are a blessing in our lives, we share God's love with others.

It is important for families to live in hope. This Advent we can celebrate being the people of God by giving praise to God for all our blessings. Let us reach out to others. We can take time to tell people in our lives what they mean to us. What a great way to begin the Church year.

Advent question

✦ What are some blessings for which our family can give thanks to God?

Advent activity

Think of ways to thank people who are a blessing to our family. This might be a teacher, family friend, or people who went out of their way to help us. We can call on the phone, write a note, or send an email. We can also include a special note in a Christmas card thanking someone for being a blessing in our lives. What are some other ideas? Let's make plans to do these things during this Advent season.

Advent prayer

God of all blessings,
during this Advent season we praise you
for sending Jesus Christ to us.
We thank you for the many blessings
you have given to our family
and for your love for each of us.
Teach us to be grateful for all your gifts
and to share what we have been given.
Amen.

Long for the Lord

Advent reflection

Do you like it when you get another chance to do something right? During Advent we have another chance to live as we were created, as people of love and patience.

Sometimes we are not patient people. We want things now. But if we did not have the four weeks of the Advent season, we would miss so much. This season helps us remember that we are waiting, not for the gifts under the tree, but for the Lord who comes as a Savior for all.

We can help bring Christ to others during Advent by our caring and patient actions. We all want love in our lives. During Advent we find that what we are longing for was here all along. We only had to open our hearts and our lives to others to discover God's love for each of us.

Advent question

✦ What is one way our family can bring God's love to others during Advent?

Advent activity

Start a new family tradition for Advent. Contribute to an organization that makes a difference in the lives of others. The amount does not have to be large. In fact, you don't have to give money at all. Sometimes the best contribution is the gift of our time in service to our neighbors. Sit down as a family and decide together which charity to support. After you make your gift of love, remember to pray for the people in need in our world with the prayer below.

Advent prayer

God of all nations,
during this holy Advent season
we wait in hope for the coming of Jesus.
Help us remember that Jesus came
for all nations and all people.
May our family work together
to bring about your kingdom.
Come, Lord Jesus.
Amen.

Embrace the Season of Wonder

Advent reflection

Have you ever been really surprised? God goes beyond all expectations and sends us a Savior who is the Son of God. What a wonderful surprise! Our God is an awesome God who loves us. God is greater than we could ever imagine.

Advent is a season of wonder as we reflect on all that God has done for us. We wait in hope to celebrate the child in the manger who is the Savior on the cross. We reflect on all that the coming of Jesus Christ means to us and to our world.

Our family must follow the way of love that Jesus Christ showed us. We must reach out to other people because each of us is created in God's own image. We must love others in God's name because in that way we give praise to God. We can share the gifts God has given us as a family with others during this season of wonder.

Advent question

✦ What are some ways we can reach out to others this Advent?

Advent activity

Imagine what the world would be like if we lived Advent each day. People would live in peace, we would share with others so no one was in need, and we would praise God together each day. If we use our imaginations, we can get a glimpse of how God created our world to be. Then we can work toward making a reality.

Talk about what the world would look like if everyone saw Jesus in others each day as a family. Share your thoughts and ideas with one another. What are some ways our family can make this a reality?

Advent prayer

God of all people,
we give thanks and praise to you
for all you have done for us.
During this Advent season,
may our family find ways
to share your love with others.
Amen.

26

Bible Search

We prepare for the coming of Jesus during the season of Advent. We get ready in our hearts and our lives to celebrate all that Jesus Christ means to us. We are called to share God's love with others through our words and actions. The reading from Isaiah that we hear during Advent reminds us to get ready for the coming of the Lord.

Work together as a family to fill in the blanks with the words from Isaiah 40:3–5. Use the words below. Then read the passage aloud together. These verses speak to our lives today and our faith in Jesus Christ.

In the desert _ _ _ _ _ _ _ the way of the LORD!

Make _ _ _ _ _ _ _ _ in the wasteland

a highway for our God!

Every valley shall be _ _ _ _ _ _ in,

every mountain and _ _ _ _ shall be made low;

the rugged _ _ _ _ shall be made a plain,

the rough country, a broad _ _ _ _ _ _ .

Then the glory of the _ _ _ _ shall be revealed.

land   **straight**

valley   **filled**

prepare   **hill**

LORD

Word Find

The readings of the second Sunday of Advent help us to walk our journey through the Advent season. We wait in hope to celebrate the coming of Jesus in a manger in Bethlehem. We are called to share that hope with others.

At the bottom of this page are words from the readings of the second Sunday of Advent. Work together as a family to find and circle as many words as you can. Hint: letters can be used in more than one word.

S	P	I	R	I	T	O	F	L	Z	B	I	C	R	A	X
L	R	O	G	O	P	N	C	H	R	T	W	I	Y	Z	P
J	E	S	U	S	B	P	R	O	P	H	E	T	Q	L	H
A	P	E	A	C	E	A	R	P	T	T	L	U	A	J	E
R	A	R	L	W	A	I	T	E	V	Y	C	Z	L	N	C
F	R	S	B	A	P	T	I	S	M	I	O	R	O	R	S
M	E	R	C	Y	W	F	H	G	J	T	M	P	C	T	I
L	I	K	I	N	G	D	O	M	R	L	E	Q	D	Y	A
R	C	F	L	U	P	S	B	T	L	Z	I	O	L	Z	E

KINGDOM	PEACE	SPIRIT
HOPE	PREPARE	WAIT
JESUS	BAPTISM	WAY
WELCOME	MERCY	PROPHET

28

Third Week of Advent

The Gospels this week begin to get us ready for the coming of Jesus. John the Baptist is a messenger sent by God to share the good news of Jesus with others. As we listen to John's message, we must learn to live our faith in Jesus Christ with joy.

Being followers of Jesus is not something added to our lives. Jesus shows us how we are called to change our whole lives to follow him.

"This is the one about whom it is written:

Rejoice in the LORD always.
PHILIPPIANS 4:4

'Behold, I am sending my messenger ahead of you; he will prepare your way before you'" (Matthew 11:10).

John was a witness to Jesus. He prepared the way. This is a good week to look at the preparations we are making in our lives for the celebration of the coming of Jesus Christ at Bethlehem. We should see if we are getting ready with elaborate decorations and parties or if we are getting ready by making more

29

time for prayer and sharing with others.

Are we preparing for Jesus' coming in the right way?

"A man named John was sent from God. He came for testimony, to testify to the light, so that all might believe through him" (John 1:6–7).

Light is a powerful image for us. Our whole world depends on the light of the sun. We, too, need Jesus as the light of the world to show us the way to the Father. We are to turn toward the light of Jesus Christ.

How can we become people of the light this Advent and testify to the light in our lives?

"John said to them in reply, 'Whoever has two tunics should share with the person who has none. And whoever has food should do likewise'" (Luke 3:11).

John reminds the people of God that we are to share with one another. We were created for life in a community. We need each other. We are to look beyond our wants to the needs of other people. Jesus shows us by his teaching and his example that we are to be people who care about others. We are to share what we have with other people so they will have what they need.

What are some ways we can share what we have with others?

Share God's Love

Advent reflection

Did you ever get a gift that you really liked? The season of Advent is a wonderful gift in our lives. It is an opportunity to live in love and share God's love with others.

God created us with loving hearts to reach out to others. But sometimes we fail to share God's love. We should take the opportunity this Advent season gives us to share the resources of the world God created for us. Only then are we living as God created us to be.

We are called to follow the example of Jesus Christ and to share God's love. We can do this by having compassion for other people. Through our words, our actions and our prayers we serve others as Jesus Christ did, and we make a difference in our communities and in our world.

Advent question

✦ How can we share God's love today?

Advent activity

This Advent we can reach out a helping hand to someone who is struggling. This time of year can be difficult for people who face celebrating Christmas without a loved one or who are seriously ill.

Let's talk about ways our family can bring hope to the life of at least one person during this Advent season. Some ideas include: visiting the elderly or those in a nursing home, inviting a family friend without any loved ones nearby to our Christmas celebrations, or sending a card or letter to support someone who is struggling this season. Together we can choose one idea and do it together this week.

Advent prayer

God of faith, hope, and love,
we thank you for this Advent season
with all its endless possibilities
Strengthen our family to live in your love
by being people of compassion each day.
Guide our hearts and our lives
as we seek to share your love with others.
Amen.

Make a Difference

Advent reflection

Do you ever think that what you do doesn't seem to matter to others? Each of us is important to God. And each of us can make a difference in the lives of others.

As Christmas draws closer, we should take a look at how we are living the season of Advent. We should look for opportunities to show compassion for people in need, even when we have troubles of our own. We can offer a helping hand, even when we think we don't have the time. We can share God's love, even when we want to keep it all to ourselves.

People sometimes think that what we do will never make a difference, but it does. One step at a time, one person at a time, we can change the lives of others. With God all things are possible.

Advent question

✦ How can our family make a difference in the life of another person during Advent?

Advent activity

Reach out to welcome someone who is new to your parish. Invite another family to participate in an Advent activity in your home or at your parish. In this way you can help new people connect with others in your parish, community, neighborhood, or school.

Advent prayer

Father of us all,
during the holy season of Advent
we give you glory and praise.
Help our family get ready to celebrate
the coming of Christ at Christmas.
May we share the spirit of hope
of this season with others.
Amen.

Share the Good News

Advent reflection

Do you share good news with others? John the Baptist shared the good news that Jesus was coming. We should do that, too.

During Advent we prepare for the coming of Jesus Christ. As a Church we point the way to Christ for others. We show others what we believe by what we choose to do with our time and energy. We should look at how we live the season of Advent to see if what we believe about this season is reflected by our actions.

The true meaning of Christmas is not gifts and parties, but a manger and a star. The child born in a stable was the Savior of the world. We are called to make Christ visible to others by the way we live our lives. This Advent we can walk the way to Bethlehem and Christmas with love for God and love for others.

Advent question

✦ How can other people see Christ through us?

Advent activity

As a family, set up a manger scene to remember the good news we are getting ready to celebrate. Talk about God's love for us. Then review the Christmas story by reading from the Gospel (Luke 2:1–19) and put the figures into place one by one as they are named. Add Mary, Joseph, and baby Jesus in a manger. Then place the shepherds in the scene. They were the first witnesses of the Christmas miracle.

Advent prayer

Lord Jesus Christ,
help us to tell others the good news
as John the Baptist did.
Give our family the courage to follow you
and to welcome others in your name.
May we witness to your love for all people
in all we do and say each day.
Amen.

Explore the Season of Possibilities

Advent reflection

Do you ever think about how things could be different in your life? The season of Advent is one of endless possibilities.

During Advent we are called to reach out to others in the name of Jesus. We remember those who feel forgotten, people who struggle with illness, and those living in poverty. We must see Jesus Christ in others.

We can use our imaginations to see the possibilities for making our lives better and our world a better place. At Christmastime we see what our lives can be if we lived in faith, hope, and love all through the year. This season, rightly lived, should set us on a journey that lasts beyond the Advent season. In this way we will we get a glimpse of the kingdom of God and help to make it a reality in our world.

Advent question

✦ What are some possibilities we see for changing our lives and our world?

Advent activity

This Advent we should look beyond our own lives to learn about people in need in other parts of our world. This helps us expand our understanding of the difficult conditions that many families face in our world today. Awareness is the first step toward action.

As a family, talk about an article or Internet site that gives us a global vision of our world by teaching us about events and problems in other countries that we don't know or think about. How can we help meet their needs? Always remember that prayer is a good first step.

Advent prayer

Holy Spirit of love,
during this holy Advent season
we know that you are with our family
as we gather together in prayer.
Through you, Jesus Christ lived among us and
redeemed the world. Help our family to share hope
in Jesus Christ now and always.
Amen.

Let God Work Through Us

Advent reflection

Is it easy to say yes when we are asked to do something? Mary must have been afraid when the angel brought her God's message. She certainly didn't plan on seeing an angel in the midst of her day.

But Mary said yes to God. She let God work through her to bring a Savior to the world. We also must cooperate with what God has in mind for us. We, too, must have the courage to say yes to God's plan.

Mary gave praise to God for all that has happened in a prayer we call the Magnificat. This is also our prayer. God has done great things for us. We, too, should proclaim the greatness of God to others and rejoice in God. God can do great things in our family if we allow God to work through us.

Advent question

✦ How can our family let God work through us?

Advent activity

What we cannot do on our own, we can do with God's help, if we let God work through us. As a family, let's talk about how we can be open to God's presence. It can be tough to find God, especially if we are going through a difficult time. What are some challenges we have faced recently, as a family or as individuals? How can we open our hearts and lives to God's love and begin to heal? How can we remember that God is always with us?

Advent prayer

God, Father of us all,
we thank you for Mary, who said yes
that she would be the mother of Jesus.
May we also do your will in our lives,
even when we find it difficult.
Strengthen our family to overcome
the challenges in our lives
that we may give glory to you.
Amen.

Wait in Joyful Hope

Advent reflection

Do good things take time? The prophet Isaiah kept hope in a savior alive for people many years before Jesus came. He asked people to be faithful to God, who was always faithful to them. The people of Israel waited for thousands of years for a redeemer to come. It was hard, but they did not lose hope in God. Then God fulfilled the promise in a way that no one could ever have expected.

We sometimes see Advent as a time for a long list of things to do to get ready for Christmas. We forget to make time for what is important. This Advent we can try to keep the reason for the season before us. We wait in joyful hope because we know the rest of the story. God has kept the promise made to the people and to us. Jesus is coming!

Advent question

✦ What is your favorite Advent or Christmas tradition?

Advent activity

Sometimes we act as if everything depends on us and forget about what is really important. Instead of trusting God, we hurry around trying to do it all.

This year, let's choose as a family to keep only the Christmas traditions that family members find meaningful. Or, we can begin a special new tradition that keeps Christ as the focus of our family celebrations.

Advent prayer

God of glory,
we thank you for keeping the promise
you made to your people.
We praise you for sending Jesus to us
as a child at Christmas and a Savior at Easter.
Help our family get ready to celebrate Christmas
in all we say and do.
Amen.

Trust in God

Advent reflection

Did you ever do the right thing when it was difficult? That is what Joseph did. He followed what God wanted him to do and trusted in God's plan. He must have been a person of great faith and courage. God would have chosen such a person to take care of Jesus.

We should follow the example of Joseph and do the right thing regardless of what people may think of us. God has been faithful to the promises that God made to the people. We are called to be faithful to God.

We seem to be people who worry too much about what other people think. We want the same clothes as other people, the same electronics, and the same car. This Advent season, let's try to be mindful of what God thinks of us and what God expects of us.

Advent question

✦ Why is it important to care more about life with God than the opinion of others?

Advent activity

God gives us hope, even when life is difficult. We don't know what the future will bring, but we know God will be with us always. God is our Creator, and each of us has been given gifts and talents to share with one another.

Talk as a family about trusting God in all things. What does it mean to trust God? Why is it hard to trust God when we want to be in control?

Advent prayer

God of hope,
during this Advent season,
fill our hearts with faith
and our lives with your love.
Help our family have the courage
to do what is right, as Joseph did.
May we be faithful to you
in all times and places of our lives.
Amen.

Bible Search

Advent is a season of prayer and a season of sharing God's love with others. We rejoice during Advent because we are getting ready to celebrate the coming of Jesus. God loves us with an unending love, and the proof is that he sent his Son. Scripture helps us to remember that we were created for life with God and that we are to rejoice in Jesus Christ our Lord.

The reading from 1 Thessalonians that we hear on the third Sunday of Advent reminds us to rejoice. Work together as a family to fill in the blanks with the words in this reading, which is found in the Bible at 1 Thessalonians 5:16–18, 23. Use the words below.

Rejoice always. __ __ __ __ without ceasing,

In all circumstances give __ __ __ __ __ __ ,

for this is the will of __ __ __ for you in Christ Jesus.

May the God of __ __ __ __ __

himself make you perfectly holy

and may you entirely, __ __ __ __ __ __ , soul, and body,

be preserved blameless for the __ __ __ __ __ __

of our Lord Jesus Christ.

coming   **thanks**

peace   **God**

spirit   **pray**

Word Find

The readings of the third week of Advent help us to give praise to God for all that God has done for us. We are reminded of our call to share the good news of Jesus Christ with others.

At the bottom of this page are words from the readings of the third Sunday of Advent. Work together as a family to find and circle as many words as you can. Hint: letters can be part of more than one word.

B	R	E	J	O	I	C	E	W	L	O	R
E	L	W	I	T	N	E	S	S	T	W	P
L	A	C	E	G	H	T	H	A	N	K	S
I	Z	P	R	O	C	L	A	I	M	X	O
E	G	O	O	D	A	P	R	A	I	S	E
V	S	J	E	S	U	S	E	N	R	Z	C
E	F	A	I	T	H	F	U	L	U	R	U
N	A	T	I	O	N	S	C	Q	D	I	J
Z	F	P	L	X	C	V	E	S	L	E	O

WITNESS	JESUS	PRAISE
NATIONS	SHARE	REJOICE
PROCLAIM	GOOD	GOD
BELIEVE	THANKS	FAITHFUL

Fourth Week of Advent

The Gospels this week center on how God works through people. These Gospels tell us the stories of Joseph, Mary, and Elizabeth, who co-operate with God's plan for the Chosen People. They are an example of faith for all of us.

"The angel of the Lord appeared to him in a dream and said, 'Jo-seph, son of David, do not be afraid to take Mary your wife into your home. For it is through the holy Spirit that this child has been conceived in her'" (Matthew 1:20).

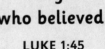

Blessed are you who believed.

LUKE 1:45

We see that Joseph does the will of God by going ahead with his marriage to Mary. He places his trust in God, even though he is worried. We, too, are to trust in God in the difficult times of our lives. It makes all the difference.

How can we better show we trust God even in difficult times?

"[The angel says to Mary:] 'And behold, Elizabeth, your rela-tive, has also con-ceived a son in her old age...for nothing will be impos-sible for God.'

40

Mary said, 'Behold, I am the hand-maid of the Lord. May it be done to me according to your word'" (Luke 1:36–38).

Mary has questions for the angel, but she agrees to do God's will. We, too, are to say yes to what God asks of us. Nothing is impossible with God, and God's plan is always for our benefit.

What seemingly impossible things has God done for us in our lives?

"Elizabeth, filled with the holy Spirit, cried out in a loud voice and said, 'Most blessed are you among women, and blessed is the fruit of your womb. And how does this happen to me, that the mother of my Lord should come to me'" (Luke 1:41–43)?

After the angel leaves her, Mary goes to visit cousin Eliza-beth, who is pregnant with John the Baptist. When Mary arrives at Elizabeth's house, Elizabeth greets her with joy. The words of Elizabeth to Mary become part of the Hail Mary prayer that we pray today to honor Mary. Elizabeth opens her heart and her life to God's will for her. We should do the same, living our call to be Advent people just like Elizabeth.

How can we open our hearts to God?

See Jesus in Others

Advent reflection

Is there someone in your life who always helps you? Jesus sent the Holy Spirit to help each of us. During Advent we can pray to the Holy Spirit to fill our hearts with love for God and love for others.

All around us are people who struggle to get through each day. We should reach out to people who are sick, lonely, or living in poverty. We are called to bring the good news of Jesus Christ to these people who are struggling and to remember that every person is made in the image of God.

Sometimes we fail to see the presence of Jesus Christ in others. We think because they are a different generation from us, a different economic status, or a different culture that they do not have anything to teach us. But they have much to teach us if only we open our lives and hearts to them.

Advent question

✦ How do we see God's presence in our lives and in those around us?

Advent activity

As we walk through the busy days at the end of the Advent season, let's take a deep breath. As a family, we can take time to stop and remember what we are getting ready to celebrate. Why is Christmas really important? Let's make a list of the most important things we need to do to prepare for Jesus' coming as a family. We can post this list where we will all see it and be reminded of what we must do to celebrate the coming of Christ at Christmas.

Advent prayer

God, you are Father, Son, and Holy Spirit.
We give praise to your holy name
as our celebration of Christmas draws near.
Renew our hearts and our lives
and fill them with your love.
May our family share your love with others
in all that we do during Advent.
Amen.

42

Hope in God's Love

Advent reflection

Have you ever been scared? We know that God is always with us, but sometimes we are still afraid.

The prophets of the Old Testament kept the hope of a savior alive, even when God's Chosen People were afraid. The prophets called the people to be faithful to God, because God is a God of hope. God fulfilled the promise in a way that we could never have imagined. God's Son came to us as teacher and Savior.

We, too, are called to trust God in our lives. During Advent we look forward to the celebration of Christmas. This season is not so much about what we do but about what God has done for us. We remember all that God has done for us as individuals and as a family. We have much for which to be thankful this season, especially for God's love for each of us.

Advent question

✦ How do we know that God loves us?

Advent activity

Create Christmas ornaments as a reminder that the Jesus of the manger is the Jesus of the cross. If your family has Christmas cards from last Christmas, cut those with a nativity scene into crosses. If not, print images of nativity scenes from the Internet, or draw your own. Punch a hole in the top and thread a length of ribbon through it to hang on the tree. These are simple, meaningful ornaments for the Christmas tree.

Advent prayer

God of love,
we thank you for your unending love
for each of us and for all people.
Help us to always remember
that you are with us each day.
May we have trust in you
even when people are against us.
We put our hope in you.
Amen.

Open Our Hearts

Advent reflection

Did you ever help someone who really needed it? Advent is a time to open our hearts to the needs of others. We are called to bring the light of God's love to other people by what we say and do. We are called to be signs of hope in our world.

Advent is a wonderful season, filled with the hope and promise of Christmas. Sharing God's love brings hope to people for whom life is filled with difficulties. We are called to bring Christ into the world for those who are poor, sick, refugees, lonely, grieving, and all who find life a challenge. When we reach out and make time for others during the Advent season, we open our hearts to them and share our hope in Jesus.

Advent question

✦ Who do we know that needs our family's help?

Advent activity

We can open our hearts to the needs of people around us. As a family, let's talk about ways we can do this. For example, we can take time to really listen when someone needs to talk, or offer encouraging words to someone who is facing difficulties. What are some other ways we can help people in our community and in our world who face difficult times? Let's choose one of these actions and do it.

Advent prayer

Lord Jesus Christ,
we know that you came to teach us
about the Father's love for all people.
During this season of Advent,
help our family live in love for one another.
May we open our hearts and reach out
to others in your name.
Amen.

Take Time to Remember

Advent reflection

Did you ever forget something? God never forgets us. God will never turn away from us and will always be with us. We can always trust our God, because our God is a God of unending love.

During Advent we remember all that God has done for us, and we look forward to the celebration of Christmas as a family. We know that our God fulfilled the promise made to God's people to send a Savior. God's own Son came to us as teacher and Savior.

We have much for which to be thankful for this season, especially for God's love for each of us. It is important to remember all that God has done for us and share God's love with others in the name of Jesus Christ our Lord.

Advent question

✦ What is one way our family can thank God for all that God has done for us?

Advent activity

When your family puts up your Christmas tree, make it a party. Have hot chocolate and candy canes. Play Christmas music. Make this a great family time and not something that *has* to get done. Invite others to share in this family tradition.

Advent prayer

Amazing God,
thank you for your love
for each one of us.
You are faithful to the promises
you made to your people.
During this season of Advent,
may our family live in joy
because you are with us always.
Amen.

Turn Toward God

Advent reflection

Is there someone in your life you trust? We can always trust God because God is an awesome God. Even when we are not faithful, God never turns away from us.

During Advent we remember how God has been faithful to people throughout the ages. Through the power of the Holy Spirit, God the Father sent Jesus Christ to us as our Savior. Jesus showed us how we are capable of living as God's creation, and he proved to us that we can always trust God.

This Advent turn toward God. Remember what it is we are really celebrating: the coming of Jesus. We turn together toward the light and love of Christmas. In this way we discover the life for which we were created by God.

Advent question.

✦ In these last days of Advent, what are some ways can we turn toward God?

Advent activity

Even on days when everything seems to go wrong, we can find something for which to give thanks and praise to God. We can think about the world God made and how God loves us with an unending love. Let's try to think of ten things for which we can thank God as a family. One family member can write down our list. Then, we can pray in thanksgiving to God for our blessings.

Advent prayer

God, Father of all people,
we thank you for sending Jesus
to us as Savior and Redeemer.
May we turn our hearts and our lives
toward you this Advent season.
Empower our family to share your love
with others as Jesus did.
Amen.

Talk to God

Advent reflection

Do you ever feel lonely? God is here with us always. God never goes away from us. We can talk to God anywhere and any place, and God always hears our prayers.

Our awesome God calls us to rejoice that Jesus Christ came to show us how to live and to redeem us through his death and resurrection. We should celebrate that we are never alone.

The Advent season offers us a wonderful opportunity to live our faith as people of prayer. Prayer is an important part of our relationship with God and should be woven through the fabric of our lives. In prayer we lift up our hearts to the God who created us and loves us.

Advent question

✦ What is one way our family can pray together during Advent?

Advent activity

This Christmas consider giving the family a gift to share. Together we can talk as a family about some gifts we would like to share. Possible examples include a fun afternoon of bowling, a trip to a children's museum, or an outing to a park. Cut out a picture of where you are going and wrap it up. Put the gift under the tree to be opened on Christmas morning. Even if it is not a surprise, it will be fun for everyone to share the excitement of gift-giving and gift-opening.

Advent prayer

Creator God,
we lift up our hearts and our prayers to you
during this holy season of Advent.
Our family rejoices and gives you thanks
for all that you have done for us.
Strengthen us to give glory to your name
in all we say and do this day.
Amen.

Be People of Hope

Advent reflection

Do we ever lose hope in difficult situations? The prophet Isaiah was the greatest prophet of the Old Testament. He kept hope of a redeemer alive for the people of Israel. He reminded them that God is faithful to the covenant God made with the people.

We, too, wait in hope during Advent to celebrate our Lord Jesus Christ. Jesus came for all people: past, present, and future. We look back to his coming as a child in Bethlehem, and we look forward to his coming again at the end of time.

It is important to be examples of hope for others, especially for those who find this time of year difficult. We can help people find comfort in God's unending love for each of us. The gift of hope is one of the greatest gifts that we can share with others.

Advent question

✦ Why is hope an important gift for someone who is struggling during Advent?

Advent activity

Family members can have fun together making a colorful paper chain to use as a Christmas decoration. Cut strips of red and green construction paper or patterned scrapbook paper and fasten them into interlocking circles using a stapler. Each family member can make a section of the chain and then combine the sections together. Find a great place to display your chain at home, such as across a mantle or the top of a window.

Advent prayer

God of hope, as we live the season of Advent,
open our hearts to the needs of others
who are having a difficult time.
May we share hope and love
with others in your holy name.
Help us remember that you are with us
at all times, places, and seasons of our lives.
Amen.

Bible Search

During Advent we remember that Mary said yes to God. She agreed to be the mother of God's own Son. She did God's will, even though she had to know that this would be difficult and change her life forever. We, too, are called to say yes to God in our lives during Advent. We honor Mary for her role in bringing Christ into the world as a human person and as an example for all of us.

Work together as a family to fill in the blanks with the words in this reading from Luke 1:34–38. Use the words below.

But Mary said to the _ _ _ _ _ , "How can this be...?"

And the angel said to her in reply,

"The holy _ _ _ _ _ _ will come upon you,

And the _ _ _ _ _ of the Most High will overshadow you.

Therefore the _ _ _ _ _ to be born will be called holy,

the Son of God. And behold, Elizabeth, your relative,

has also conceived a _ _ _ in her old age...

For nothing will be impossible for _ _ _ .

_ _ _ _ said, "Behold, I am the handmaid of the Lord."

May it be done to me according to your _ _ _ _ ."

child	**word**
God	**Spirit**
power	**son**
angel	**Mary**

49

Word Find

The readings of the fourth Sunday of Advent help us to remember that Jesus, God's own Son, came as a child to be one of us. He showed us how we are capable of living as God's creation.

At the bottom of this page are words from the readings of the fourth Sunday of Advent. Work together as a family to find and circle as many words as you can. Hint: Letters can be part of more than one word.

A	Q	F	P	C	D	X	B	R	P
G	C	W	O	Y	A	L	A	Z	O
S	G	O	W	R	S	O	N	L	R
F	O	R	E	V	E	R	G	I	J
C	S	D	R	B	R	D	E	S	K
H	P	A	T	C	V	Z	L	T	Y
I	E	T	A	F	A	T	H	E	R
L	L	I	V	E	N	S	G	N	B
D	P	V	U	C	T	Q	J	R	Z

FOREVER	SON	WORD
LORD	GOSPEL	LISTEN
FATHER	CHILD	LIVE
POWER	SERVANT	ANGEL

Family Prayer

Loving God,
as we journey through the Christmas season,
we know that we walk with you.
You bring hope and joy to our lives
through your Son, our Lord Jesus Christ.

Fill our hearts with your love that we may
support one another in our family.
Guide us to treat each other with respect,
dignity, and care as your creation.

Give our family the strength to face
any challenges that will come our way.
We know that you are with us always,
and through you all things are possible.

Help us as a family to reach out to others
and find a way to help people in need.
We remember that we bring Christ
into the world for others by sharing your love.

We ask you to bless our family.
May we be living signs of your presence
by the way we live our lives each day
of the Christmas season and beyond.

Amen.

First Week of Christmas

The season of Christmas begins with our celebration of Christmas Mass. This is a season to share God's love and to rejoice at the coming of Jesus Christ. During Christmastime we are called to look beyond ourselves to see the needs of others. We are called to be Christ for other people. As we live the spirit of the Christmas season, we catch a glimpse of what is possible for our world.

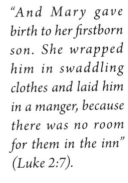

Glory to God in the highest.

LUKE 2:14

"And Mary gave birth to her firstborn son. She wrapped him in swaddling clothes and laid him in a manger, because there was no room for them in the inn" (Luke 2:7).

Each year at midnight Mass on Christmas Eve, the story from Luke 2:1–14 is proclaimed. We hear again of

Mary and Joseph traveling to Bethlehem and the birth of Jesus in a humble stable. This story of God's unending love brings hope to our lives.

What new lesson can we learn from the Christmas story this year?

"So the shepherds went in haste and found Mary and Joseph, and the infant lying in the manger. When they saw this, they made known the message that had been told them about this child. All who heard it were amazed" (Luke 2:16–18).

At Mass at dawn on Christmas Day, the story of the shepherds is proclaimed. They believe what the angel tells them and go to see the child who is a Savior. Then they tell others and they give praise to God. We, too, are called to believe in the Christmas miracle and give praise to God in our lives.

How can we tell others about the joy of Christmas?

"...What came to be through him was life, and this life was the light of the human race; the light shines in the darkness..." (John 1:3–5).

At the other Masses on Christmas Day, the Gospel is from John 1:1–18. We hear proclaimed that Jesus is the Word of God. This Gospel reading reminds us that the Son of God existed for all eternity. Jesus Christ came to us as the light of the world. He came for people of all nations and all times.

What are some ways that we can walk in the light of Jesus in our lives today?

Go On a Journey to Bethlehem

Christmas reflection

What is your favorite thing to do on Christmas? Each year all of us are called again to Bethlehem. We come as did the shepherds to see a Savior. We come as did the angels to give glory to God. We come together to hear once more this wonderful story.

We joyfully celebrate the birth of the Christ child because we know the rest of the story. The child in the manger is the teacher, the Messiah, and the Savior of all people. Such is the love of God for us.

This Christmas let us share our joy and love with others as we come together to celebrate the birth of Jesus Christ. As we begin this holy Christmas season, may the love of God fill our hearts and the joy of the coming of Jesus Christ fill our lives.

Christmas question

✦ How does Christmas help us remember what is important in life?

Christmas activity

Read together from the Gospel of Luke the story of the first Christmas (Luke 2:1–19). Share this story as a family at home as the first thing you do before your Christmas celebration begins. Before the gifts, before the food, before launching into the day, remember what we celebrate on Christmas.

Christmas prayer

God, Father, Son, and Holy Spirit,
on this wonderful Christmas Day
our family celebrates all that you have done for us.
Out of love you sent Jesus Christ
to be born as a child in Bethlehem for all people.
In the spirit of Christmas giving,
help our family to live our faith in you each day.
Amen.

Give Glory to God

Christmas reflection

Were you ever surprised when someone came to visit unexpectedly? The shepherds must have been really surprised the night Jesus was born. They did not expect to see angels while they were taking care of their sheep.

At Christmas we sing the Gloria as we proclaim, "Glory to God in the highest." The words of the angel from Luke's Gospel become our words, too. Together we lift up our voices, our hearts, and our lives to the God who loves us and sent Jesus to us.

For many families the first day of the Christmas season is the end of their celebration. The tree goes out to the curb, and Christmas carols no longer play on the radio. But the feast of Christmas is too great to be celebrated in a single day. We are called to give glory to God throughout the Christmas season, not only on December 25.

Christmas question

✦ What are some ways that we can offer glory to God?

Christmas activity

During the Christmas season, we are called to look at how we are living our lives and find ways to share the love of God with others. Let's talk about ways to do this as a family. What are some ways our family can make a difference in our world? Choose one action to begin during this Christmas season.

Christmas prayer

Creator God,
we give you glory and praise
for all that you have done for us.
We thank you for the gift of your Son,
our Lord Jesus Christ.
May our family bring hope to others
during this holy Christmas season.
Glory to God in the highest!
Amen.

Make Room in Our Hearts

Christmas reflection

Have you ever been really tired? That's how Mary and Joseph must have felt after their long journey. The Gospel of Luke tells how they tried to find a place to stay but were turned away. There was no room for them to stay in the inn.

The Christ child was born in a humble stable. This reminds us that what is important is not what kind of house we have or the clothes we wear. It is who we are on the inside that really matters.

This Gospel calls us to make room for Jesus Christ in our lives. Sometimes we fill our days with so many activities that we don't make room for doing God's will. This Christmas season let's see Christ in others. Let's be Christ to others. Let's make room for Christ to come again.

Christmas question

✦ How can we make room in our hearts and lives
   for other people?

Christmas activity

In the days after Christmas many families have some time off from school and jobs. Find opportunities to serve others as a family. Visit someone in a nursing home, do a chore for an elderly neighbor, or make a simple meal for someone who is homebound. What are some other ways to help people in the local community?

Christmas prayer

God, Father of all people,
we lift up our hearts to you in prayer
this holy Christmas season.
We thank you for sending Jesus Christ
to show us your unending love for us.
May we make room in our hearts
and lives for people in need.
Amen.

Live in the Light

Christmas reflection

Do you ever feel you are too busy with everything you have to do? This Christmas season is a good time to make choices about priorities in our lives. We are called to follow the light of Christ each day. Our choices should reflect what is really important in our lives.

We know that God is always here with us. Sometimes we move ourselves further from God in choices we make, but God never moves away from us. We must turn away from the darkness and toward the light of God's love.

The Christmas season invites us to walk in the light of Jesus Christ. We can leave behind whatever has kept us from living fully as God's people and followers of Jesus Christ. We can choose to use our time for what really matters. This can be a time of new beginnings in our lives. Let us walk into the light of God's love and live always in the light.

Christmas question

✦ What does it mean to live as followers of Jesus each day?

Christmas activity

Gather as many family members as are available and play a board game or card game together. If a family member received a new game for Christmas, play that one. Otherwise choose a favorite game or one that you haven't played in a while. Focus on just enjoying being with one another. Perhaps a Christmas-season game night can be a new tradition for your family.

Christmas prayer

God of light,
hear our prayer this Christmas season
and be with our family in all that we do.
Empower us to follow Jesus Christ
and to live always as his disciples.
May we live always in the light
and show your light to others.
Amen.

Share the Joy of Christmas

Christmas reflection

Do you ever think that Christmas is over too soon? Christmas Day is only the beginning of the Christmas season. We continue to celebrate the coming of Jesus into our world and our lives.

During Christmas we experience the love and joy of the season in many ways. We spend time with family and friends. We open our hearts and our lives to people in need.

When Christmas Day is over, the real work of Christmas is just beginning. It can be a time of miracles as people put aside their differences to work together. We cannot put our Christmas spirit away with the Christmas decorations. The goodwill and love toward others that we shared at Christmas must continue.

Christmas question

✦ What gifts and talents can we share with others?

Christmas activity

Look at Christmas cards sent by far-away family members. Talk about favorite memories of some of these relatives. Also share some funny stories. Laugh together. This helps families feel connected even if far apart in miles. Family stories bind people together and help family members feel that sense of belonging which is so important.

Christmas prayer

God of love,
we thank you for all of creation
and for your love for each of us.
Help our family to share your love
with other people in our world.
May we reach out a helping hand
in the name of Jesus Christ our Lord.
Amen.

Learn From the Surprises of Christmas

Christmas reflection

Has something good ever happened to you when you weren't expecting it? The wonderful season of Christmas is one filled with surprises for all of us.

First is that the Savior was born in a stable. Not a house, but a place where animals were kept. Then shepherds on the hillside were visited by an angel. And magi journeyed from the East to bring gifts to the Christ child. Who could ever have imagined this!

The surprises of the Christmas season teach us an important lesson—that we must be open to the unexpected in our lives. We must look for Jesus in all people and places. Be open to new people, new experiences, and new ways of looking at things. Be open to the experience of loving God and others in unexpected ways.

Christmas question

✦ Where do we find God in unexpected places?

Christmas activity

It is important for us to open ourselves to experiencing God's love in new ways this Christmas. We are also called to broaden our understanding of what it means to live in a global community. Make plans as a family to go to a festival or performance that celebrates people of another culture. This is a fun family activity and helps us see that our differences enrich our world.

Christmas prayer

God of surprises,
we thank you for the gift of Jesus,
which is more than we could imagine.
Help us to be open to your presence
in our lives and in one another.
May we look in unexpected places
to experience your love for all people.
Amen.

Share the Love of Jesus for All People

Christmas reflection

Did you ever have something you didn't want to share with anyone else? That's not how it is with Christmas. Christmas is for people of all ages, people of all races, and people in all walks of life. Christmas is for everyone because Jesus Christ came for all people.

At Christmas we celebrate the child in the manger who grew up to be the Savior on the cross. We know all that the coming of Christ means to the world because we know the rest of the story. Jesus loves us so much that he died and rose for us!

We rejoice that Jesus taught us about God's love for each of us and how we are to share the love with others. We are called to follow Jesus in our lives with the help of the Holy Spirit.

Christmas question

✦ How do we share the love of Jesus with others today?

Christmas activity

Think about ways your family can make a difference in the lives of others. Possibilities include making time to be with others by watching one less TV show or making one less cell phone call. Then look for opportunities each day to do these small things that can make a big difference. In this way we can together walk into the new calendar year and live with faith, hope, and love for God and other people.

Christmas prayer

Lord Jesus Christ,
we give you thanks for all you have done,
and for showing us the way to the Father.
Help us to follow your way of love
and to live with compassion for others.
Send your Holy Spirit to guide our family
in all we do today and always.
Amen.

Bible Search

The Gospel reading about the shepherds is proclaimed during the Christmas season. The wonderful story of the shepherds who hear the good news of a Savior is one that is forever in our memories. The first visitors to the Christ child were shepherds because Jesus came for all people. How surprised they must have been and how filled with joy at the message from God!

Work together as a family to fill in the blanks with the words in this reading from Luke 2:8–11. Use the words below.

Now there were shepherds

in that region living in the _ _ _ _ _ _ and

keeping the night watch over their _ _ _ _ _ .

Then angel of the Lord appeared to them and

the _ _ _ _ _ of the Lord shone around them,

and they were struck with great _ _ _ _ .

The _ _ _ _ _ said to them, "Do not be afraid;

for behold, I proclaim to you good news

of great _ _ _ that will be for all the people.

For today in the city of David a _ _ _ _ _ _

has been born for you

who is Messiah and _ _ _ _ .

joy   **glory**   **fear**

angel   **Savior**   **Lord**

flock   **fields**

Word Find

Christmas is a time to remember what is important and to celebrate how good God is to us. Each year we hear the story from Luke that will forever change the world. We live in hope because of the love of God for each one of us.

At the bottom of this page are words from the Christmas Gospels. These words speak to us of the joy we have because of the coming of Jesus for all of us. Work together as a family to find and circle as many words as you can. Hint: letters can be part of more than one word.

G	L	O	R	Y	S	Z	J	L	Z	S
A	P	W	U	C	L	F	I	A	L	H
B	E	T	H	L	E	H	E	M	X	E
M	A	R	Y	Q	M	C	K	A	C	P
X	C	J	O	S	E	P	H	Z	T	H
Z	E	N	G	T	E	B	S	E	F	E
L	R	I	N	N	D	G	O	D	Q	R
L	O	R	D	C	S	Q	N	F	N	D
Y	V	Z	M	A	N	G	E	R	I	S

INN	GOD	BETHLEHEM
MARY	SON	GLORY
SHEPHERDS	MANGER	PEACE
JOSEPH	AMAZED	LORD

Second Week of Christmas

The Gospels of the Christmas season call us to faith in Jesus Christ. As the Gospel writers looked back on the event at Bethlehem, they saw the meaning of the child born in a stable. They knew that this child would grow up to forever change the world and would be the Savior of us all. His humble birth reminds us that it is not what we have,

We saw his star at its rising and have come to do him homage.

MATTHEW 2:2

but who we are that is important in life.

"They returned to Galilee, to their own town of Nazareth. The child grew and became strong, filled with wisdom; and the favor of God was upon him" (Luke 2:39–40).

The feast of the Holy Family is about showing us that family life is holy because it is life with God. The family of Jesus, Mary, and Joseph went through hard times, but they were faithful to God's will for their lives. They lived their faith in their everyday lives. We are to support and encourage one another on our faith journey.

How can we be faithful to God's will for our family, even when it is hard?

"All who heard it were amazed by what had been told them by the shepherds. And Mary kept all these things, reflecting on them in her heart" (Luke 2:18–19).

On the great feast of Mary, the Mother of God, we hear again from the Gospel of Luke the story of the shepherds on that first Christmas. Mary is faithful to God and lives her promise to be the mother of the Savior. Throughout her life she kept saying yes to God.

What are some ways we can become more like Mary?

"And behold, the star that the magi had seen at its rising preceded them, until it came and stopped over the place where the child was" (Matthew 2:9).

On Epiphany we celebrate that Jesus came for all people and all nations. We are one people, enriched by our differences and united in the love of God for all people. All people are to follow Jesus as the star of their lives.

What does it mean to follow Jesus as the star of our lives?

Honor Mary

Christmas reflection

Is it ever hard to do something you said you would do? Mary had faith in God even though she faced struggles in her life. She and Joseph had to go to another country to keep Jesus safe. When Jesus grew up, she saw people turn against him. She stood at the foot of the cross and saw her son suffer.

Each year we celebrate the feast of Mary, Mother of God, one week after Christmas. We remember that because Mary said yes to God, she helped bring Christ into the world as a Savior for all people. We honor her as the mother of Jesus and the mother of all of us.

Mary is a sign of hope in our world. We should follow her example and say yes to God. And of course, we can ask Mary to pray for us to her Son.

Christmas question

✦ How can our family be faithful to God even in times of trouble, like Mary was?

Christmas activity

Mary is the Mother of God and our mother, too. The story of Mary giving praise to God is in Luke 1:46–55. This prayer of Mary is called the Magnificat. We, too, are called to give praise to God for all that God has done for each of us and for our family. As a family, let's read aloud Mary's prayer from the Bible.

Christmas prayer

Awesome God,
today we celebrate Mary,
Mother of Jesus and our mother, also.
Give us the courage to say yes
to God's plan for our lives as she did.
May we follow the example of Mary,
and give praise and glory to you
for all that you have done for us.
Amen.

Celebrate God's Love

Christmas reflection

What is your favorite Christmas carol? As we sing the wonderful words of our favorite Christmas songs, we are reminded of what Christmas is all about. We celebrate that God came to us in the person of Jesus Christ that we might live in love of God and others.

The Christmas season is a time to rejoice. Our celebration of the birth of the Christ child opens our hearts to the unending love of God for each of us. The true gift of the Christmas season is the gift of love, given to us and shared with others. What a wonderful gift this is.

We are united in love as one family of God, despite our differences. We should see our many cultures and traditions as enriching our lives and our world. Let us live in love throughout the Christmas season and throughout our lives.

Christmas question

✦ What can we learn from people of different cultures?

Christmas activity

Christmas carols tell the Christmas story in song and help us celebrate the coming of Jesus in beautiful ways. As a family, sing carols at Mass and at home, or listen to CDs of your favorites. Help younger children learn the words to carols such as "Away in a Manger" and "Silent Night."

Christmas prayer

God of wonder,
in the joy of the Christmas season
we give you thanks for our blessings
and for all that you have done for us.
Help us remember that our
traditions and cultures enrich us all.
Be with our family in all that we do
that we may give honor to your name.
Amen.

Proclaim the Gospel Today

Christmas reflection

Did something so wonderful ever happen to you that you could hardly wait to share it with others? The disciples of Jesus felt that way. They shared the good news of Jesus Christ with others. They went far and wide preaching the Gospel.

Each of us hears the good news of Jesus Christ from other people. In this way our faith in Jesus Christ is handed on from generation to generation. The faith of each person enriches us all because we are the family of God.

We are called to share our faith in Jesus Christ with other people. The news is too good to keep to ourselves. Through our words and actions, we show others what it means to believe in our Lord Jesus Christ.

Christmas question

✦ Who shares the good news about Jesus with us?

Christmas activity

Share time as a family looking at pictures of family members when they were younger. This is a fun activity and helps family members feel connected to one another and remember the good times. Share stories about the good times you had with one another and point out those people who have taught you about Jesus.

 ### Christmas prayer

God of Christmas joy,
we give you thanks for sending us
your Son, our Lord Jesus Christ.
We ask that you fill our lives with your joy
and our hearts with your love for others.
May our family share the good news
with other people in the name of Jesus.
Amen.

See the Possibilities

Christmas reflection

What do you think the world would be like if everyone lived as Jesus showed us? Christmas gives us a glimpse of what is possible. As people reach out to one another, we see what our world might be like if we lived the season of Christmas in our lives each day.

We are called to love one another as we love ourselves. This means we should love all people, not just people we like or people who are easy to get along with. We are to expand our idea of loving others as we grow in faith during the Christmas season.

By loving others, we make them aware of God's love and presence in the world. We walk in the footsteps of Jesus Christ.

Christmas question

✦ How can we see the face of Jesus Christ in other people?

Christmas activity

Talk as a family about how we are called to live in love as disciples of Jesus Christ. Even during the hard times, we are called to show God's love to others by being loving people. Although we cannot choose what happens to us, we can choose how we respond. We can either allow difficulties to make us want to strike back at people, or we can let our experiences prompt us to help others.

Together, make a list of some ways we can choose to do the right thing in daily life. Post this list somewhere where all family members can see it and be reminded to live in love to build a better world.

Christmas prayer

Holy Spirit of love,
through you the Son of God
became human like us.
Help our family to live our faith each day
and to work for justice for all people.
May we be people of prayer in all things
and people of love toward others.

Amen.

Live the Gospels

Christmas reflection

Are we called to help people in need, or is that for others to do? As we open our hearts to the wonders of Christmas, we realize that we are called to live the challenge of God's word. Our faith should make a difference in how we live our lives. We must love one another as God loves us.

Around our world children still die of hunger, people's lives are shattered by violence, and the desperation of poverty overwhelms the lives of others. We must care about what happens in our world and do something about it. The same God is the Creator and Father of all people.

Because of our faith in God, we are called to look beyond ourselves to see the needs of others. Christmas should make a difference in our lives and, through us, in the lives of other people.

Christmas question

✦ How would our world be different if everyone lived
the message of the Gospels?

Christmas activity

We are called to live in compassion, forgiveness, and love. In following the example of Jesus, we live how God created us to live. It is a challenge to live as Gospel people. As a family, discuss what it means to be disciples of Jesus. Think of ways we can make a difference during the Christmas season and beyond.

Christmas prayer

Amazing God,
we ask you to give us hearts filled with love
and compassion for all people.
Help our family to love you and love others.
Grant us the courage to make a difference
in our world for other people.
Amen.

Share the Miracle of Christmas

Christmas reflection

Have you ever seen a miracle? There are miracles that happen every day. We can see a miracle in each unique snowflake, in the vivid colors of blooming flowers, in the smile of a baby, and when people from different traditions come together to give praise to God.

The greatest miracle of Christmas is the love of God for each of us. God sent a Savior to us. And the miracle does not end with Christmas, rather it is just beginning. Our God is an awesome God.

The Gospels show us the compassion of Jesus for others. We, too, are called to love others and to be compassionate like Jesus. We can look for ways to help people in need in our world. People sharing God's love with others is another miracle of Christmas.

Christmas question

✦ What are ways we can show compassion for others?

Christmas activity

Many people around our world suffer from poverty, drought, war, discrimination, sickness, and hunger. Pray together as a family for people in need of hope so they will know that God is with them always. Pray also that other people will open their hearts to them and will make a difference in their lives.

Christmas prayer

God of all nations,
we give glory and praise to you
for the miracle of love that is Christmas.
Help our family to have compassion for the sick,
as Jesus showed us by his example.
Open our hearts to the needs of other people,
not just during the Christmas season
but throughout the year.
Amen.

Act As a Peacemaker

Christmas reflection

Do you think one person can make a difference? Each of us is called to make a difference in our world by living in love and peace. God blesses us to help us live our faith. We are called to be a blessing to others.

God made people of different cultures and different races. All of us are God's creation and called to life with God and with one another. We must remember that each of us is created in God's own image and likeness.

With the help of the Holy Spirit, we can witness to the meaning of the Christmas season in our lives. All nations and all cultures can work together to build the kingdom of God for all people. Then the story of love of the Christmas season will become a reality in our lives and our world.

Christmas question

✦ How can we act as peacemakers in our lives?

Christmas activity

The needs of others continue long after Christmas. Take time to look at ways your family can serve people in need in the community. If your parish collects items for a food pantry, for example, put it on your calendar for the next scheduled date. Consider how you might continue to live the spirit of Christmas giving in the new year, and make a plan to do so.

Christmas prayer

God of peace,
we rejoice in the gift of Jesus Christ,
who taught us about your love.
Help our family follow his example
and witness to your love each day.
May we work for justice in our world
for all nations, all cultures, all people.
Amen.

Follow the Star

Epiphany reflection

Have you ever been amazed at all the stars in the sky? The magi studied the stars. When they saw a bright new star, they followed it to Jesus. They traveled a long way, and the journey must have been difficult.

The feast of Epiphany is celebrated each year on the second Sunday after Christmas. We hear the story of the magi, and it reminds us that Jesus came for everyone.

Just like the magi, we should recognize the star of Jesus Christ in our own lives. We should be open to where the star leads, even when we are busy, even when we face challenges, even when it isn't easy. Each day we are called to step out into the light and follow the star of Jesus Christ.

Epiphany question

✦ How can we follow the star of Christ in our lives?

Epiphany activity

We are called to bring hope to the lives of others near and far during the Christmas season and beyond. As a church we observe National Migration Week beginning on Epiphany. We remember migrant workers and refugees who try to make a better life for their families. This week is set aside to appreciate the diversity of people. Check the U.S. Bishops Web site at usccb.org for ideas for your family observance for this week.

Epiphany prayer

Lord Jesus Christ,
help us to be like the magi
who followed the star to find you.
May we also seek you with an open heart
and look where you will be found.
Guide us to follow your star in our lives
in all times and places.
Amen.

Bible Search

The feast of Epiphany celebrates the fact that Jesus came for all people and all nations. The story of the magi is a story for our lives, too. They followed the star to find Jesus and honor him. We, too, must follow the star in our lives to Jesus.

Work together as a family to fill in the blanks with the words from this reading from Matthew 2:9–11. Use the words below.

After their audience with the _ _ _ _ ,

the magi set out.

And behold, the star that they had _ _ _ _

at its rising preceded them

until it came and stopped over the place

where the _ _ _ _ _ was.

They were overjoyed at seeing the _ _ _ _ ,

and on entering the house

they saw the child with _ _ _ _ his mother....

Then they opened their treasures

and offered him _ _ _ _ _

of _ _ _ _ , frankincense, and myrrh.

child   **gifts**

gold   **Mary**

star   **king**

seen

Word Find

On Epiphany we celebrate our joy that Jesus Christ has come for all people. We give thanks to God with the words of Psalm 72 as we sing out praise to God. We join our voices with the voices of people the world over in giving thanks to God.

At the bottom of this page are some words from this psalm. Work together as a family to find and circle as many words as you can. Hint: letters can be used in more than one word.

C	P	G	S	O	N	Q	M	N	Z	C
P	E	O	P	L	E	B	R	H	X	E
K	A	D	D	A	Y	S	L	R	D	S
R	C	J	K	P	K	J	X	I	B	A
H	E	C	G	O	I	U	Z	U	A	R
N	A	T	I	O	N	S	A	C	Q	L
T	L	X	F	R	G	T	D	M	Y	M
Q	B	R	T	I	Y	I	M	P	V	R
V	Z	Y	S	W	L	C	A	L	L	D
S	E	R	V	I	C	E	O	I	T	H
U	O	S	L	E	A	B	O	C	G	J

SON	KING	POOR	SERVICE
GOD	PEACE	JUSTICE	CALL
NATIONS	PEOPLE	DAYS	GIFTS

74

Saints and Feasts for the Advent and Christmas Seasons

The lives of the saints provide examples of faith for us. Saints lived the Gospels in many different ways. They were real people who faced real difficulties in following Jesus. But they were faithful to God and God's purpose for their lives. God has a purpose for each of us, too.

There are many ways for our families to celebrate Advent and Christmas saints. We can learn how they lived. We can talk about how they are examples for our lives. We can choose a project to do as a family that helps us be like a saint. We can have a celebration to honor a saint. We can ask the saints to pray for us to God.

Some of the saints we celebrate during the season of Advent are:

Saint Francis Xavier ✦ December 3

Francis was born in Spain to a rich family. Francis knew that God was calling him to share the Gospels with others. Francis prayed to God about what he should do. He became a missionary and went to India and Japan to tell the people there about Jesus. We, too, are called to share the good news.

✦ Why is prayer important in our lives?

Saint Nicholas ✦ December 6

Nicholas was a bishop long ago. He loved others as Jesus asks us to do. Nicholas liked to help people in secret. He often gave candy or small toys to children. His spirit of generosity is an example to all of us during the Advent season.

✦ How can we share with others like Saint Nicholas?

Immaculate Conception of Mary ✦ December 8

We celebrate this holy day during the season of Advent. We remember that Mary was without sin from the first moment of her life. We honor Mary's example of faith. She said yes to God even when she knew it would change her life.

✦ How can we say yes to God in our lives?

Our Lady of Guadalupe ✦ December 12

Mary appeared to a poor man named Juan Diego on his way to Mass in Mexico. She told him to ask the bishop to build a church for the people. Juan went to the bishop and the bishop asked him for a sign. When Juan opened his cloak, there was an image of Mary on the fabric.

✦ How can we have faith in difficult times?

Saint Lucy ✦ December 13

This young saint lived long ago. Her name means light. Her feast day was originally celebrated when the days started getting longer. Lucy was always a person of courage and prayer. She followed the way of Jesus even when many around her did not understand.

✦ Why does it take courage to follow Jesus?

Saint Mary Di Rosa ✦ December 15

She served Jesus by seeing his face in people who were poor. She set up a house for girls from poor families so they had a safe place to sleep. She also took care of people who were in the hospital. Mary Di Rosa did whatever she could to help others.

✦ How can we help people in need during Advent?

Saint Peter Canisius ✦ December 21

He was a teacher and a book author. Peter Canisius proclaimed the word of God to others. He also cared for the sick during an epidemic. People liked to come and hear him preach the Gospel. He was a very busy person who did all he could to teach people about God.

✦ What are ways we can tell others about Jesus?

Saint John Kanty ✦ December 23

This learned person was a great teacher. Some people were envious of him and had him fired from his job. It was a difficult time for John, but he tried to serve God in whatever he did. Later, he taught Scripture to university students to help them learn about God's word.

✦ How can we live the word of God in our lives?

Some the saints and feasts we celebrate during the Christmas season are:

Saint John the Apostle ✦ December 27

This apostle was a fisherman like Peter. Jesus called John and his brother, James, to follow him. John was a person of great faith in Jesus. John did not run away, but stayed at the foot of the cross. He preached the good news of Jesus Christ far and wide.

✦ How can we follow Jesus even when it is difficult?

Saint Caterina Volpicelli ✦ December 28

This recently canonized saint was from a well-to-do family. As a teen she thought mostly about dances and the theater. Then she decided to devote her life to Jesus Christ. Caterina helped other people and opened a home for children without parents. She was also a person of prayer.

✦ Who are people for whom we can pray?

Feast of the Holy Family

We celebrate the Holy Family of Jesus, Mary, and Joseph on the Sunday between December 25 and January 1. In the years when no Sunday occurs between those dates, this feast is celebrated on a weekday. Family life is sacred, not because families are perfect, but because God works through families to help them live in love of God and one another.

✦ How can family members show support for one another?

Mary, Mother of God ✦ January 1

We celebrate that Mary, in her role as the mother of Jesus, is the Mother of God. She said yes to God and is an example of faith for all of us. She was a faithful disciple of Jesus who stood at the foot of the cross and was in the upper room. We can ask Mary to pray for us to her Son.

✦ What is your favorite Mary song?

Holy Name of Jesus ✦ January 3

On this day we celebrate that the child born in a stable was named Jesus. This is the name that the angel told Joseph to name the child because this child would save the people. Joseph did as the angel had asked. We remember that Jesus is God and that his name is sacred.

✦ How can we honor the name of Jesus?

Saint Elizabeth Ann Seton ✦ January 4

She was a widow with five children. When she became a Catholic her friends turned against her and would not talk to her. This hurt her very much, but she knew she was doing the right thing. Elizabeth was a teacher. She started a school and taught children about God.

✦ How can we help children in our community?

Saint Charles Houben ✦ January 5

One of the newly canonized saints, Charles Houben loved God and others. This priest had great faith in God, and many people came to seek his blessing. He was a person of great compassion. Charles visited the sick and dying in the hospital and at home.

✦ How can we help people who are sick?

Epiphany ✦ January 6

This feast celebrates the coming of the magi from the East to honor Jesus and bring him gifts. We remember that Jesus came for all people and all nations. The twelve days of Christmas is the time between Christmas and Epiphany. Now that this feast is celebrated on a Sunday, the number of days varies.

✦ How can we treat people of other cultures with respect?

Bible Search Solutions

1st Week of Advent

ways   teach   truth
God   wait   Lord
love

2nd Week of Advent

prepare   straight
filled   hill   land
valley   Lord

3rd Week of Advent

pray   thanks   God
peace   spirit   coming

4th Week of Advent

angel   Spirit   power
child   son   God
Mary   word

Christmas

fields   flock   glory
fear   angel   joy
Savior   Lord

Epiphany

king   seen   child
star   Mary   gifts
gold

Word Find Answer Key

FIRST WEEK OF ADVENT

```
C E S G R P C U H R O C M X Y U
A U R L I G H T G J Z T G O D S
T W H E A R T S L O N K L Q U N
J E S U S E D G N U P E O P L E
S S N B N R C F B R V S R K O P
I O P C O M I N G N X I Y T R G
G N I A W E S O M E K S I L N S
N L A W A K E G B Y L O R D O Q
S N R B G I Z L Q P O L P U R T
```

FOURTH WEEK OF ADVENT

```
A Q F P C D X B R P
G C W O Y A L A Z O
S G O W R S O N L R
F O R E V E R G I J
C S D R B R D E S K
H P A T C V Z L T Y
I E T A F A T H E R
L L I V E N S G N B
D P V U C T Q J R Z
```

SECOND WEEK OF ADVENT

```
S P I R I T O F L Z B I C R A X
L R O G O P N C H R T W I Y Z P
J E S U S B P R O P H E T Q L H
A P E A C E A R P T T L U A J E
R A R L W A I T E V Y C Z L N C
F R S B A P T I S M I O R O R S
M E R C Y W F H G J T M P C T I
L I K I N G D O M R L E Q D Y A
R C F L U P S B T L Z I O L Z E
```

CHRISTMAS

```
G L O R Y S Z J L Z S
A P W U C L F I A L H
B E T H L E H E M X E
M A R Y Q M C K A C P
X C J O S E P H Z T H
Z E N G T E B S E F E
L R I N N D G O D Q R
L O R D C S Q N F N D
Y V Z M A N G E R I S
```

THIRD WEEK OF ADVENT

```
B R E J O I C E W L O R
E L W I T N E S S T W P
L A C E G H T H A N K S
I Z P R O C L A I M X O
E G O O D A P R A I S E
V S J E S U S E N R Z C
E F A I T H F U L U R U
N A T I O N S C Q D I J
Z F P L X C V E S L E O
```

EPIPHANY

```
C P G S O N Q M N Z C
P E O P L E B R H X E
K A D D A Y S L R D S
R C J K P K J X I B A
H E C G O I U Z U A R
N A T I O N S A C Q L
T L X F R G T D M Y M
Q B R T I Y I M P V R
V Z Y S W L C A L L D
S E R V I C E O I T H
U O S L E A B O C G J
```